T0113514

IN HIS Presence

JOURNAL

JOANNE MALBROUGH

authorHOUSE®

AuthorHouse™
1663 Liberty Drive
Bloomington, IN 47403
www.authorhouse.com
Phone: 833-262-8899

Published by AuthorHouse 07/30/2021

ISBN: 978-1-6655-3262-4 (sc)
ISBN: 978-1-6655-3261-7 (e)

Dedication

First, I want to give thanks and praise to God our Father for giving me the determination to complete this project and to have published my first journal book. Without His help, His strength, and His wisdom, I could not have done it. Second, I want to dedicate this journal to my handsome sons, Darnell and Joshua Malbrough, for being my motivation and my heart; to my parents, Leon and Mary Robert for their love, prayers, encouragements, and continual support; to my siblings: Brenda Robert, Shirley Kla- Williams, Lilly [her husband, Timothy Broussard], Adam [his wife, Debrica Robert], Merry Robert, Paul [his wife, Ebony Robert], Eric [his wife, Mariah Robert]; to my dear friend and Sister in Christ, Brandy Moore, for her prayers and encouragements; to my church family in Lafayette, Louisiana for their love and prayers; and to all who congratulated me and wished me the very best as I was working on this journal. God bless you. I appreciate you all so much. I pray that it blesses you as much as it has blessed me creating it.

Enjoy spending time with the Father! This journal is between you and God.

Much love,
JoAnne

A huge thank you and credit to:
GOD, The CEO of All Things Possible

Perry Steward:
CEO of 2 Lee Graphic Visions & Digital Video, LLC
Designed:
Book Cover
Copyright Release
Mini Photo Session
Facebook Cover
Social Media Meme

Brandy Moore
Hair and Make-up for Photo Shoot

Introduction

"In His Presence Journal" will allow you to write your most intimate prayers and petitions, thoughts, decrees, and declarations as you spend quiet time in the presence of God. At the top of every other page you will read scriptures from various Bible versions and scripture verses that you can meditate on. You will also see some of my inspirations and words of encouragement as well.

As you allow God into your heart, feel His perpetual love and sweet embrace. God wants a relationship with you, and He wants you to spend time with Him. Sometimes it may become a bit difficult and overwhelming to put thoughts and prayers into words. Writing them down is another way in which you can communicate with God. He knows your deepest thoughts anyway; and He knows what you are in need of before you even ask it of Him.

Remember the prayer that our Lord and Savior Jesus taught us to pray in Matthew Chapter 6:9-13, KJV:

"Our Father, which art in heaven,
Hallowed be Thy name.
Thy kingdom come. Thy will be done in earth, as it is in heaven.
Give us this day our daily bread.
And forgive us our debts, as we forgive our debtors.
And lead us not into temptation, but deliver us from evil:
For thine is the kingdom, and the power, and the glory, for ever. Amen"

"...My presence will go with you, and I will give you rest."
[Exodus 33:14, ESV]

Inspiration: God will always go before you. When you put your complete trust in Him, He makes it known that He is with you and that you will never walk alone. If you are facing a trying moment right now, remember that Your Heavenly Father's presence is with You and the peace that only He can give will rest upon your heart.

Date:_____

_____

_____

_____

_____

_____

_____

_____

_____

_____

_____

_____

_____

_____

*Date:*_____

_____

_____

_____

_____

_____

_____

_____

_____

_____

_____

_____

_____

_____

_____

_____

_____

_____

_____

_____

_____

_____

_____

"Create in me a clean heart, O God; And renew a right spirit within me. 11. Cast me not away from thy presence; And take not thy Holy Spirit from me."
[Psalm 51:10-11, ASV]

Inspiration: God wants you to serve Him with a clean heart. You can go before God and ask the Father to give you a heart that will glorify Him. You must empty yourself and allow the Holy Spirit to do a work on the inside of you that will please the Father. God promised that He will not fail you nor forsake you as mentioned in Deuteronomy 31:6. Because the Holy Spirit now lives on the inside of you, God's holy presence is always with you.

*Date:*_____

_____

_____

_____

_____

_____

_____

_____

_____

_____

_____

*Date:*_____

_____

_____

_____

_____

_____

_____

_____

_____

_____

_____

_____

_____

_____

_____

_____

_____

_____

_____

_____

_____

"God, I invite Your searching gaze into my heart. Examine me through and through; find out everything that may be hidden within me. Put me to the test and sift through all my anxious cares." [Psalm 139:23, TPT]

Inspiration: You can invite the Father into your heart knowing that He loves you with an everlasting love. God cares and He will never leave you in a place of darkness. God knows your hearts and your every thought. Nothing is hidden from Him. If you submit your heart to God, He will help you by sifting those things that are not of Him out of you.

Date:_____

_____

_____

_____

_____

_____

_____

_____

_____

_____

_____

_____

*Date:*_____

_____

_____

_____

_____

_____

_____

_____

_____

_____

_____

_____

_____

_____

_____

_____

_____

_____

_____

_____

_____

_____

"Humble yourselves in the presence of the Lord, and He will exalt you." [James 4:10, NASB]

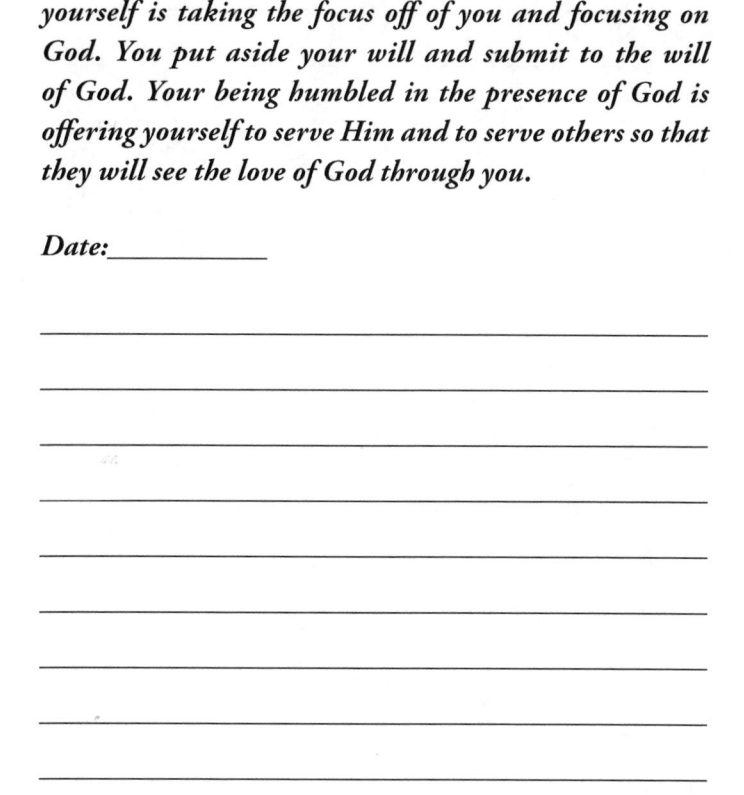

Inspiration: Your daily walk with the Father is to humble yourself.....to know that it is not about you, but all about God. You do not glorify yourself, but God. To humble yourself is taking the focus off of you and focusing on God. You put aside your will and submit to the will of God. Your being humbled in the presence of God is offering yourself to serve Him and to serve others so that they will see the love of God through you.

*Date:*_____

_____

_____

_____

_____

_____

_____

_____

_____

_____

_____

_____

*Date:*_____

_____

_____

_____

_____

_____

_____

_____

_____

_____

_____

_____

_____

_____

_____

_____

_____

_____

_____

_____

_____

_____

"Let go [of your concerns]! Then you will know that I am God. I rule the nations. I rule the earth." [Psalm 46:10, GWT]

Inspiration: Whatever it is that you are facing, let go and let God. He knows how to handle every situation. He wants you to trust Him, to be still and know that He is God. If you are able to let go of your concerns or whatever it may be, you will be able to let God because you trust Him to give you the answer that you need.

*Date:*_____

_____

_____

_____

_____

_____

_____

_____

_____

_____

_____

_____

*Date:*_____

_____

_____

_____

_____

_____

_____

_____

_____

_____

_____

_____

_____

_____

_____

_____

_____

_____

_____

_____

_____

_____

"How lovely is Your dwelling place, LORD Almighty! 2. My soul yearns, even faints, for the courts of the LORD; my heart and my flesh cry out for the living GOD."
[Psalm 84:1-2, NIV]

Inspiration: When you spend time with God by meditating on His Word, by talking with God, and by taking time to pray, God will embrace you with His beautiful presence. You will stand in awe of God. You will want more of Him and desire to spend even more time with Him. You will see the beauty of being in His presence.

Date:_____

_____

_____

_____

_____

_____

_____

_____

_____

_____

_____

Date:_____

_____

_____

_____

_____

_____

_____

_____

_____

_____

_____

_____

_____

_____

_____

_____

_____

_____

_____

_____

_____

"Come close to God, and God will come close to you. Wash your hands, you sinners; purify your hearts, for your loyalty is divided between God and the world." [James 4:8, NLT]

Inspiration: When you come close to God, He will come close to you. God will not force His will on you. He loves you, and He wants to help you be the person that He called you to be. When you become a born again believer, you will see that the Blood of Jesus has washed you and purified you. God has thrown your sins into the sea of forgetfulness. So do not be afraid to go before the Father. When you draw close to God, you will start to let go of the cares of this world and start doing the things of God. Come closer... He will not push you away.

Date:_____

_____

_____

_____

_____

_____

_____

_____

_____

*Date:*_____

_____

_____

_____

_____

_____

_____

_____

_____

_____

_____

_____

_____

_____

_____

_____

_____

_____

_____

_____

_____

_____

"I am the vine; you are the branches. If you remain in me and I in you, you will bear much fruit; apart from Me you can do nothing." [John 15:5, NIV]

Inspiration: You belong to God and He is your Father. Know that you can do nothing in and of yourself without the help of the Father. You will be fruitful as long as you stay connected to Jesus.

*Date:*_____

_____

_____

_____

_____

_____

_____

_____

_____

_____

_____

_____

_____

*Date:*_____

_____

_____

_____

_____

_____

_____

_____

_____

_____

_____

_____

_____

_____

_____

_____

_____

_____

_____

_____

_____

"Where can I go from Your Spirit? Or where can I flee from Your presence?" [Psalm 139:7, AMP]

~~~~~

Inspiration: God has a plan and a purpose for your life. He knows what He has destined for you, and He wants you to come to know it so you can fulfill it. Even if you tried running a million miles away or tried hiding underneath the smallest rock, God knows exactly where you are. If God wants to use you for such a time as this, you will eventually stop running from Him and allow Him to use you unto His glory.

*Date:*_____

_____

_____

_____

_____

_____

_____

_____

_____

_____

_____

*Date:*_____

_____

_____

_____

_____

_____

_____

_____

_____

_____

_____

_____

_____

_____

_____

_____

_____

_____

_____

_____

_____

"Now the Lord is the Spirit, and where the Spirit of the Lord is, there is liberty [emancipation from bondage, true freedom]." [2 Corinthians 3:17, AMP]

∞

Inspiration: There is no place you can go so deep where God cannot reach you. Where His presence is, there is such freedom that no man can give. God sets you free from whatever it is that has you bound... {the things of the spirit, soul, and body}. There is true liberation from God. He wants to set you free from every form of bondage. Trust God....call upon Him...He alone can truly set you free.

Date:_____

_____

_____

_____

_____

_____

_____

_____

_____

_____

_____

*Date:*_____

_____

_____

_____

_____

_____

_____

_____

_____

_____

_____

_____

_____

_____

_____

_____

_____

_____

_____

_____

_____

_____

"Let us come before His presence with thanksgiving, and make a joyful noise unto Him with psalms." [Psalm 95:2, KJV]

Inspiration: God gets all the glory, honor, and praise ...He so deserves it. You cannot deny that He has been so good to you. So when you go before God in prayer, before you ask Him of anything, begin to praise Him. Begin to let the Father know just how much you are so thankful for who He is and for all that He is to you. Begin to thank Him for all that He has done for you and for all that He continues to do.

Date:_____

_____

_____

_____

_____

_____

_____

_____

_____

_____

_____

*Date:*_____

_____

_____

_____

_____

_____

_____

_____

_____

_____

_____

_____

_____

_____

_____

_____

_____

_____

_____

_____

_____

_____

"One thing that I have asked of the Lord, that will I seek, inquire for, and [insistently] require: that I may dwell in the house of the Lord [in His presence] all the days of my life, to behold and gaze upon the beauty [the sweet attractiveness and the delightful loveliness] of the Lord and to meditate, consider, and inquire in His temple."
[Psalm 27:4, AMPC]

Inspiration: You will not find in all the earth anything more beautiful than the presence of the Lord. To be in His presence is like the beauty of heaven's doors open wide for you. In this world there is always some kind of test or some kind of trial you might go through in your life. But when you meditate on the Word of the God and focus on the beauty of who God is, you will feel so much at peace... knowing that the beauty of God's presence embraces you in that very moment.

Date:_____

_____

_____

_____

_____

_____

_____

_____

*Date:*_____

_____

_____

_____

_____

_____

_____

_____

_____

_____

_____

_____

_____

_____

_____

_____

_____

_____

_____

_____

_____

"...My presence will go with you, and I will give you rest."
[Exodus 33:14, ESV]

Inspiration: You can rest assure that God keeps His promises to His children. The Father promised that His presence will go before us. So if there is something that you are dealing with and it is too heavy for you to bear, God goes before you, and He can make your pathway smooth and every crooked place straight for you. He will give you the peace that you need. Trust God and rest in Him that all is well for you.

Date:_____

_____

_____

_____

_____

_____

_____

_____

_____

_____

_____

*Date:*_____

_____

_____

_____

_____

_____

_____

_____

_____

_____

_____

_____

_____

_____

_____

_____

_____

_____

_____

_____

_____

"So repent [change your mind and purpose]; turn around and return [to God], that your sins may be erased [blotted out, wiped clean], that times of refreshing [of recovering from the effects of heat, of reviving with fresh air] may come from the presence of the Lord;" [Acts 3:19, AMCP]

Inspiration: God wants you to know that He is not punishing you, nor is He mad at you. God gives you so many chances because He loves you. He knows of every sin committed. He gives you an opportunity to repent of those sins and move forward as you renew your mind to His Word. As you take time to meditate on the Word of God, you will see that there is a refreshing of your spirit and of your mind.

Date:_____

_____

_____

_____

_____

_____

_____

_____

_____

_____

*Date:*_____

_____

_____

_____

_____

_____

_____

_____

_____

_____

_____

_____

_____

_____

_____

_____

_____

_____

_____

_____

"...There is joy in the presence of God's angels over one sinner who repents." [Luke 15:10, CSB]

Inspiration: Do you know how happy the angels are when you become a born again believer... when you receive JESUS as your risen LORD and SAVIOR? They are rejoicing over you in the very presence of your Heavenly Father. You matter to God. He is the lover of your soul. That is something to get very excited about!

Date:_____

_____

_____

_____

_____

_____

_____

_____

_____

_____

_____

_____

_____

_____

*Date:*_____

_____

_____

_____

_____

_____

_____

_____

_____

_____

_____

_____

_____

_____

_____

_____

_____

_____

_____

_____

_____

"Call on me in prayer and I will answer you. I will show you great and mysterious things which you still do not know about." [Jeremiah 33:3, NET]

Inspiration: When you go to God in prayer, He already knows what you are in need of. God says that you can call on Him and He will answer you. He is listening... even in times when you might think that He is not listening. God is the God of miracles, signs, and wonders. There is so much greater for you, and God wants to show you that. Not only does God the Father want to show you great things, He also wants to give you great things.

Date:_____

_____

_____

_____

_____

_____

_____

_____

_____

_____

_____

*Date:*_____

_____

_____

_____

_____

_____

_____

_____

_____

_____

_____

_____

_____

_____

_____

_____

_____

_____

_____

_____

"Be still and know [recognize, understand] that I am God." [Psalm 46:10, AMP]

Inspiration: Are you searching for an answer or a solution to something? Don't you wish that someone could just zap the answer in your mind? Well, God's Word has all the answers you need. He wants you to put all your trust in Him and to realize that nothing is too hard for Him. When you put your complete trust in God, just be still. He has it all figured out for you. Before you came to God in prayer with the issue, God already had the solution.

Date:_____

_____

_____

_____

_____

_____

_____

_____

_____

_____

_____

_____

*Date:*_____

_____

_____

_____

_____

_____

_____

_____

_____

_____

_____

_____

_____

_____

_____

_____

_____

_____

_____

_____

_____

"My soul thirsts for God, the living God. When shall I come and appear in God's presence?" [Psalm 42:2, BSB]

Inspiration: The more you spend time with the Father, you will want more of Him. You will come to realize that there is an even greater thirst for God. The Father knows that it is not a natural thirst but a spiritual one. It is the kind of thirst that only God can satisfy. You do not have to wait to be in His presence when you get to heaven for that thirst to be satisfied. God can quench your thirst when you are in His presence in prayer, in praise, and in worship right here in the earth. Come to the WELL that never runs dry---JESUS!

Date:_____

_____

_____

_____

_____

_____

_____

_____

_____

_____

*Date:*_____

"How I want to be there! I long to be in the LORD's Temple. With my whole being I sing for joy to the living God." [Psalm 84:2, GNT]

Inspiration: God wants to have an intimate relationship with you. It is more than just needing God. It is about wanting Him in your life and wanting Him to come into your heart. There a burning on the inside of you when you are spending time with the Father. You long to spend more time in the presence of God.....to really get to know the will of the Father concerning you. Joy will burst out....praises will be lifted up. You will surely see the beauty of His goodness.

Date:_____

_____

_____

_____

_____

_____

_____

_____

_____

_____

*Date:*_____

_____

_____

_____

_____

_____

_____

_____

_____

_____

_____

_____

_____

_____

_____

_____

_____

_____

_____

_____

_____

"We have been sprinkled [with His Blood] to free us from a guilty conscience, and our bodies have been washed with clean water. So we must continue to come [to Him] with a sincere heart and strong faith. [Hebrews 10:22, GWT]

Inspiration: How amazing is God the Father! Because of the Blood of Jesus, you have a Blood bought right to come before God without guilt, shame, or condemnation. God wants you to come to Him just as you are. His loving arms are ready to embrace you. God will never ever put you to shame, nor will He rub your sins and wrong doings in your face. He is a loving and forgiving God. Come with a sincere heart before the Father with faith to know that all that He has for you will come to pass.

Date:_____

_____

_____

_____

_____

_____

_____

_____

_____

Date:_____

_____

_____

_____

_____

_____

_____

_____

_____

_____

_____

_____

_____

_____

_____

_____

_____

_____

_____

_____

_____

_____

_____

"When You said, 'Seek My face [in prayer, require My presence as your greatest need],' my heart said to You, 'Your face, O Lord, I will seek [on the authority of Your word].'" [Psalm 27:8, AMP]

~~~

Inspiration: When you seek God with all your heart, the Father will reveal His presence to you. God desires that you would want to be in His presence. God wants you to seek Him above all else and to acknowledge Him. Since all that you are in need of stands in the very presence of God, your greatest need is GOD!

Date:_____

_____

_____

_____

_____

_____

_____

_____

_____

_____

_____

*Date:*_____

_____

_____

_____

_____

_____

_____

_____

_____

_____

_____

_____

_____

_____

_____

_____

_____

_____

_____

_____

_____

"'For I know the plans and thoughts that I have for you,'" says the Lord, "'plans for peace and well- being and not for disaster, to give you a future and a hope. 12. Then you will call on Me and I will hear [your voice] and I will listen to you. 13. Then [with a deep longing] you will seek Me and require Me [as a vital necessity] and [you will] find Me when you search for Me with all your heart.'" [Jeremiah 29:11-13, AMP]

Inspiration: When you wake up, seek the LORD. When you go throughout your day, seek the LORD. When you lay your head on your pillow, seek the LORD. With your whole entire being, seek the LORD. He will not turn His holy presence from you, nor will He turn away His love for you. God's thoughts are good toward you. God tells you that He is listening, but you must come to Him. You need God every minute, every second, and every hour of the day.

Date:_____

_____

_____

_____

_____

_____

_____

Date:_____

_____

_____

_____

_____

_____

_____

_____

_____

_____

_____

_____

_____

_____

_____

_____

_____

_____

_____

_____

_____

_____

_____

_____

"No one has ever seen God. If we love each other, God remains in us and His love is made perfect in us." [1 John 4:12, CEB]

Inspiration: The only Jesus that others will see is Jesus in you. God has placed His Spirit on the inside of you. People need to see the love of God through you. That is why you must represent Jesus as He represented the Father. Jesus represented the perfect will and love of God. His love is always on the inside of you. This is what others are longing to see in you.....the love of the Father.

*Date:*_____

_____

_____

_____

_____

_____

_____

_____

_____

_____

_____

_____

*Date:*_____

_____

_____

_____

_____

_____

_____

_____

_____

_____

_____

_____

_____

_____

_____

_____

_____

_____

_____

_____

_____

_____

_____

_____

"What bliss you experience when your heart is pure! For then your eyes will open to see more and more of God."
[Matthew 5:8, TPT]

Inspiration: How sweet it is to have your heart purified by God! It pleases God when you love Him with all of your heart. It glorifies the Father when you have a heart to love others just as the Father loves you... to have no malice or hatred in your heart for your brother or sister in Christ....to forgive quickly....to seek the will of God concerning all things....to be in perfect harmony with others of like precious faith...to keep your heart right before God... to do the things of God and to do what is pleasing unto God with all sincerity. You will see Him show up and show out in your life. You will surely see the evidence that God is present.

Date:_____

_____

_____

_____

_____

_____

_____

_____

*Date:*_____

_____

_____

_____

_____

_____

_____

_____

_____

_____

_____

_____

_____

_____

_____

_____

_____

_____

_____

_____

_____

_____

"The LORD is near to all who call on Him, to all who call on Him in truth." [Psalm 145:18, ESV]

Inspiration: God loves when His children depend on Him. God loves when you call upon Him. Although God knows exactly what you will say, He wants to hear from you. Talk to God. Hold conversations with the Father. God wants to be involved in every area of your life. He is your Creator and Father. God knows His children..... you are His child. Just as the Father is near to you, He also wants you to draw close to Him with all of your heart and soul.

Date:_____

_____

_____

_____

_____

_____

_____

_____

_____

_____

_____

*Date:*_____

"Therefore let us [with privilege] approach the throne of grace [that is, the throne of God's gracious favor] with confidence and without fear, so that we may receive mercy [for our failures] and find [His amazing] grace to help in time of need [an appropriate blessing, coming just at the right moment]." [Hebrews 4:16, AMP]

Inspiration: You can be confident and have such a boldness to approach God because the Blood of Jesus made it so. God's grace is sufficient, and He is rich in mercy. God's Holy Spirit is your Helper. God will give you the grace you need to help you in all your times of need. Call on Him and trust Him. The richness of God's grace and mercy shall forever follow you.

Date:_____

*Date:*_____

_____

_____

_____

_____

_____

_____

_____

_____

_____

_____

_____

_____

_____

_____

_____

_____

_____

_____

_____

_____

_____

"Guide me in Your truth and teach me, For You are the God of my salvation; For You [and only You] I wait [expectantly] all the day long." [Psalm 25:5, AMP]

Inspiration: It pays to wait on God. Your expectation comes from God. His Holy Spirit will guide you and lead you into all truth. God will never lead you astray nor will He set you up to fail. You can call upon the Father. He is your perfect Guide, Your Teacher, and your Savior.

Date:_____

_____

_____

_____

_____

_____

_____

_____

_____

_____

_____

_____

_____

_____

*Date:*_____

_____

_____

_____

_____

_____

_____

_____

_____

_____

_____

_____

_____

_____

_____

_____

_____

_____

_____

_____

_____

_____

_____

"The Lord your God is in your midst--- a Warrior bringing victory. He will create calm with His love; He will rejoice over you with singing." " [Zephaniah 3:17, CEB]

Inspiration: God is a Mighty God who defends you in battle. God will protect you because you are His. God will protect and depend what belongs to Him. You belong to God. The Father is your Protector. His love for you is from everlasting to everlasting. His love gives your spirit such calmness and peace. So do not worry! In Christ Jesus, you already have the victory over every situation you might face. Rejoice!! Your an overcomer and a winner!!

Date:_____

_____

_____

_____

_____

_____

_____

_____

_____

_____

*Date:*_____

_____

_____

_____

_____

_____

_____

_____

_____

_____

_____

_____

_____

_____

_____

_____

_____

_____

_____

_____

_____

_____

"If my people, which are called by my name, shall humble themselves, and pray, and seek My face, and turn from their wicked ways; then will I hear from heaven, and will forgive their sin, and will heal their land." [2 Chronicles 7:14, KJV]

Inspiration: God is calling you to pray, repent, and humble yourself. God is calling you to a life of prayer and a heart to pray about everything. In order for things to change within the earth, you need to pray. God will not do anything outside of His will and outside of prayer. If you seek God and pray, things can change in ways you never imagined.

Date:_____

_____

_____

_____

_____

_____

_____

_____

_____

_____

_____

*Date:*_____

_____

_____

_____

_____

_____

_____

_____

_____

_____

_____

_____

_____

_____

_____

_____

_____

_____

_____

_____

_____

"Seek ye the LORD while He may be found; Call on Him [for salvation] while He is near." [Isaiah 55:6, AMP]

Inspiration: God is the God of your salvation. There is nothing you did or that you can do to earn salvation. Because of Jesus, salvation is a free gift from the Father. God gives you many opportunities to seek Him...to come to Him. God loves you far to much to leave you lost and unsaved. That is why Jesus died for you and went to that cross for you. Jesus gave you access to God the Father. Jesus came to give you the abundant life that God has ordained for you to have and to live. Salvation is yours if you want it...Take it...God freely gave it to you!

*Date:*_____

_____

_____

_____

_____

_____

_____

_____

_____

_____

*Date:*_____

_____

_____

_____

_____

_____

_____

_____

_____

_____

_____

_____

_____

_____

_____

_____

_____

_____

_____

_____

_____

"But I love to stay close to God! I have chosen the Lord God to protect me. I will share all that You have done."
[Psalm 73:28, FBV]

~~~

Inspiration: Look around you and behold the beauty of God. Behold His goodness that He has shown you. God is so close to you; but if you cannot sense His presence, it could be that you are so consumed with everything else going on around you. Trust God as you go throughout your day. Remember that God does have you on His mind because He loves you. When you acknowledge God and all that He has done for you, you will surely declare His goodness.

Date:_____

_____

_____

_____

_____

_____

_____

_____

_____

_____

Date:_____

_____

_____

_____

_____

_____

_____

_____

_____

_____

_____

_____

_____

_____

_____

_____

_____

_____

_____

_____

_____

"Jesus explained, 'I am the Way, I am the Truth, and I am the Life. No one comes next to the Father except through union with Me. To know Me is to know My Father too. 7. And from now on you will realize that you have seen Him and experienced Him.'" [John 14:6-7, TPT]

Inspiration: There is no other way that you can get to the Father but through Jesus. He is the Gateway to the Father. Jesus is Truth and Eternal Life. Jesus is the true representation of the Father. If you know Him, then you also know the Father. What you see in Jesus is also in God. Man cannot get you to God... Laws cannot get you to God... Religion and traditions cannot get you to God..Politicians cannot get you to God. JESUS IS THE ONLY SURE WAY TO GOD! THERE IS JUST NO OTHER WAY!!

Date:_____

_____

_____

_____

_____

_____

_____

_____

Date:_____

_____

_____

_____

_____

_____

_____

_____

_____

_____

_____

_____

_____

_____

_____

_____

_____

_____

_____

_____

_____

"O send out Your light and Your truth, let them lead me; let them bring me to Your holy hill and to Your dwelling." [Psalm 43:3, AMPC]

Inspiration: God will make a way for you. His Holy Spirit will impart the light of truth on the inside of you. God's Word will be a lamp unto your feet and a light unto your path as stated in Psalm 119:105. As God leads you, the light of His glory brings you to a deeper place in Him.

Date:_____

_____

_____

_____

_____

_____

_____

_____

_____

_____

_____

_____

_____

Date:_____

_____

_____

_____

_____

_____

_____

_____

_____

_____

_____

_____

_____

_____

_____

_____

_____

_____

_____

_____

_____

_____

"He who dwells in the shelter of the Most High Will remain secure and rest in the shadow of the Almighty [whose power no enemy can withstand]." [Psalm 91:1, AMP]

Inspiration: You do believe that God is your Protector? You have the authority to put you, your family, and all that concerns you under the protection of the Almighty God. That secret place in God is to seek Him. You can put yourself under His protective covering and mantle. God is your divine shelter. He will not allow the enemy to snatch you out of His hand. The enemy is no match for God. You can surely rest in the shelter of the Almighty Father. He has got you covered.

Date:_____

_____

_____

_____

_____

_____

_____

_____

_____

_____

*Date:*_____

_____

_____

_____

_____

_____

_____

_____

_____

_____

_____

_____

_____

_____

_____

_____

_____

_____

_____

_____

_____

"Now without faith it is impossible to please God, since the one who draws near to Him must believe that He exists and that He rewards those who seek Him."
[Hebrews 11:6, CSB]

Inspiration: As you are writing your prayers and petitions to God, believe that God is a faithful God. He is faithful to perform that which He has promised. You must do your part....BELIEVE. Have faith in God that He will reward you because you have faith in Him.

Date:_____

_____

_____

_____

_____

_____

_____

_____

_____

_____

_____

_____

_____

_____

*Date:*_____

_____

_____

_____

_____

_____

_____

_____

_____

_____

_____

_____

_____

_____

_____

_____

_____

_____

_____

_____

_____

_____

_____

"Keep trusting in the Lord and do what is right in His eyes. Fix your heart on the promises of God, and you will be secure, feasting on His faithfulness." [Psalm 37:3, TPT]

Inspiration: How good is it to know that God is faithful to His Word and that He is faithful to perform what He has already spoken concerning you! As you mediate on His Word, know that His Word is life and spiritual food. You can be confident in this... that God will never go back on His Word. It will never return back unto Him empty. God's promises for you are YES and AMEN, as stated in 2 Corinthians 1:20. His Word will nourish you and feed your faith. His Word will fortify your faith as you meditate on it daily.

Date:_____

_____

_____

_____

_____

_____

_____

_____

_____

*Date:*_____

_____

_____

_____

_____

_____

_____

_____

_____

_____

_____

_____

_____

_____

_____

_____

_____

_____

_____

_____

_____

"Make God the utmost delight and pleasure of your life, and He will provide for you what you desire the most."
[Psalm 37:4, TPT]

⧸∞⧹

Inspiration: Delight yourself and take pleasure in God. He knows every single petition of your heart. Enjoy the Father's presence. Enjoy talking to God. Enjoy the goodness of God. Let God take His rightful place in your life as first....as the center of your joy...as your everything. Let your life be pleasing unto God. Seek to please your God Who is the One and Only True God and please Him only.

Date:_____

_____

_____

_____

_____

_____

_____

_____

_____

_____

Date:_____

"This is the confidence that we have in our relationship with God: If we ask for anything in agreement with His will, He listens to us. 15. If we know that He listens to whatever we ask, we know that we have received what we asked from Him." [1 John 5:14-15, CEB]

Inspiration: God does hear what you are saying. He does listen to your prayers. You can have total confidence and trust in God. He will not fail You. He will not disappoint you or misguide you. God is a trustworthy God. The confidence you have in Him is your faith to believe in Him... that whatever you ask of the Father, provided it is within His will, He will do it.

Date:_____

_____

_____

_____

_____

_____

_____

_____

_____

_____

*Date:*_____

_____

_____

_____

_____

_____

_____

_____

_____

_____

_____

_____

_____

_____

_____

_____

_____

_____

_____

_____

"Be still before the Lord; wait patiently for Him and entrust yourself to Him;" [Psalm 37:7, AMP]

∞

Inspiration: If you wait upon God, He will renew your strength in the waiting. God's timing is perfect. Your prayers and petitions that you present before God may not always be answered right when you want them to. But be still and wait. God will not be a second early or a second late. He knows when to release the manifestation of what you are believing Him for. It will come right on time.

Date:_____

_____

_____

_____

_____

_____

_____

_____

_____

_____

_____

_____

Date:_____

_____

_____

_____

_____

_____

_____

_____

_____

_____

_____

_____

_____

_____

_____

_____

_____

_____

_____

_____

_____

_____

"But my God shall supply all your need according to His riches in glory by Christ Jesus." [Philippians 4:19, KJV]

Inspiration: Everything that you need is in the presence of God. There is every provision in His name. There is healing, deliverance, joy, peace, strength, finances, restoration, salvation, and all that you need to live an abundant life. He is your Source and Provider. In Him you will want for nothing.

Date:_____

_____

_____

_____

_____

_____

_____

_____

_____

_____

_____

_____

_____

_____

*Date:*_____

_____

_____

_____

_____

_____

_____

_____

_____

_____

_____

_____

_____

_____

_____

_____

_____

_____

_____

_____

_____

_____

"For where two or three are gathered together in My name, I am there among them." [Matthew 18:20, CSB]

✎

Inspiration: It is good to have someone who prays with you, and you both can come together in agreement for God's will to be done in your lives. God's presence is where prayers according to His will are prayed. God's presence is where peace and harmony is. God's presence is where the Spirit of unity is. When you and someone else are praying together-- whether in person or on the phone, know that there is no distance in the Spirit. God is among you....He is there with you. In the Message Bible Translation, it states that when you get together with someone on anything at all on earth and you make a prayer of it, God goes into action. See, not only does God the Father listen to your prayers, but He also goes into action for you... so that you will see the manifestation of your prayers.

Date:_____

_____

_____

_____

_____

_____

_____

*Date:*_____

_____

_____

_____

_____

_____

_____

_____

_____

_____

_____

_____

_____

_____

_____

_____

_____

_____

_____

_____

"What joy overwhelms everyone who keeps the ways of God, those who seek Him as their heart's passion."
[Psalm 119:2, TPT]

Inspiration: To have unspeakable joy, you must follow the ways of our Lord and Savior. Jesus is the true example of pure joy. As you become more attentive to what God is saying in His Word concerning your life, you can live the abundant life that the Father ordained for you to live. It also means seeking the Father with all of your heart and soul. It is the Father's will for you to live a life of joy, peace, and prosperity in every area of your life. In God alone is where your true happiness is. Every single day, make God your passion.

Date:_____

_____

_____

_____

_____

_____

_____

_____

_____

_____

Date:_____

_____

_____

_____

_____

_____

_____

_____

_____

_____

_____

_____

_____

_____

_____

_____

_____

_____

_____

_____

_____

_____

_____

"Those who know You, Lord, will trust You; You do not abandon anyone who comes to You." [Psalm 9:10, GNT]

Inspiration: Some people may leave you or even abandon you when you need them most. Some people may not understand some of the things that you are going though. Somewhere in your lifetime, people who you thought would stay by your side will just leave. But God! God keeps His promise made to you that He will never leave your nor forsake you. Our heavenly Father will never abandon you. That is why it is important to stay in His presence...so that you will know the Father's heart...so that you will know the spoken promises He has made to you as His child...so that you will know and believe that God is always there for you, and He will embrace you right where you are.

Date:_____

_____

_____

_____

_____

_____

_____

_____

_____

Date:_____

_____

_____

_____

_____

_____

_____

_____

_____

_____

_____

_____

_____

_____

_____

_____

_____

_____

_____

_____

_____

"Seek His kingdom first, and His way of living right, and everything will be given to you." [Matthew 6:33, FBV]

∞

Inspiration: Before you go to any one else for anything, seek God. Seek the things of God. God does not want you to be dismayed, worried, or anxious about anything but to pray about it. God already knows what you need before you ask it of Him. God wants to give you the kingdom because that is His good pleasure for His children. Be in right standing with God-- always try your best to do the things of God. He will take care of you and even the things that concerns you. Never stop seeking God. Remain in His presence.

Date:_____

_____

_____

_____

_____

_____

_____

_____

_____

_____

*Date:*_____

_____

_____

_____

_____

_____

_____

_____

_____

_____

_____

_____

_____

_____

_____

_____

_____

_____

_____

_____

_____

_____

"Seek the Lord and the strength He gives! Seek His presence continually! [1 Chronicles 16:11, NET]

Inspiration: God is the strength of your life. Nothing is too hard for God to handle. God is your Strong Tower. You can lean on God. You can count on God. You can talk to God about anything. His strength is made perfect in your moments of weakness. The Father will lift your head up high with sure confidence.

*Date:*_____

_____

_____

_____

_____

_____

_____

_____

_____

_____

_____

_____

*Date:*_____

_____

_____

_____

_____

_____

_____

_____

_____

_____

_____

_____

_____

_____

_____

_____

_____

_____

_____

_____

_____

_____

"And now to Him Who can keep you on your feet, standing tall in His bright presence, fresh and celebrating— to our one God, our only Savior, through Jesus Christ, our Master, be glory, majesty, strength, and rule before all time, and now, and to the end of all time. Yes." [Jude 1:24-25, MSG]

Inspiration: Praise God that He is the One Who keeps you! He is the One Who sustains you. God is your Anchor. He is the strong foundation that you stand on. You are His child, and He will not let the enemy cause you to fall. Stay anchored and rooted in His presence. God will show forth His splendor, His glory, His strength, His majestic power in your life.

*Date:*_____

_____

_____

_____

_____

_____

_____

_____

_____

*Date:*_____

_____

_____

_____

_____

_____

_____

_____

_____

_____

_____

_____

_____

_____

_____

_____

_____

_____

_____

_____

_____

_____

_____

"You are my God. I worship You. In my heart, I long for You, as I would long for a stream in a scorching desert." [Psalm 63:1, CEV]

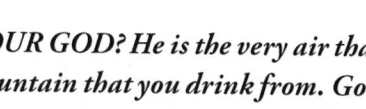

Inspiration: Is GOD YOUR GOD? He is the very air that you breathe. He is the fountain that you drink from. God is the well that will never go dry. God is your greatest necessity in order to live. He is Life. Only God knows how to fill you, refresh you, and rejuvenate you. The more you spend time meditating on His Word... the more you spend time conversing with God and getting to know the heart of the Father, you will see that you want more. You will want more and more and more and more and more of Him. God is so sweet that He will grant you your heart's desire because that is what you want..... more of Him.

Date:_____

_____

_____

_____

_____

_____

_____

_____

_____

*Date:*_____

_____

_____

_____

_____

_____

_____

_____

_____

_____

_____

_____

_____

_____

_____

_____

_____

_____

_____

_____

_____

"Pursue the Lord and His strength; seek His face always!"
[Psalm 105:4, CEB]

Inspiration: In your time of weakness, let God be your strength. You can find such joy in God being the strength of your life and the head of all that you do.

Date:_____

_____

_____

_____

_____

_____

_____

_____

_____

_____

_____

_____

_____

_____

_____

*Date:*_____

_____

_____

_____

_____

_____

_____

_____

_____

_____

_____

_____

_____

_____

_____

_____

_____

_____

_____

_____

_____

"I will answer them before they even call to Me. While they are still talking about their needs, I will go ahead and answer their prayers!" [Isaiah 65:24, NLT]

Inspiration: You can have full confidence in God that He hears your prayers, even the secret petitions of your heart. God already knows what you will say and ask of Him, but He still wants you to seek Him about the matter. Know that even if you have asked a thing of God, if it is not within His will for your life, God will not do it. What you ask of the Father has to line up with His Word.

Date:_____

_____

_____

_____

_____

_____

_____

_____

_____

_____

_____

_____

*Date:*_____

_____

_____

_____

_____

_____

_____

_____

_____

_____

_____

_____

_____

_____

_____

_____

_____

_____

_____

_____

_____

_____

_____

_____

Note from the Author

I pray that you have enjoyed scriptural readings, inspirations, and writing down your petitions, prayers, and conversations with God. This journal was written just for you. It is between you and the Father. I pray God's abundant blessings are bestowed greatly upon you, your family and your entire household. May His glory shine upon you always. May the goodness of God and the favor of God smile upon you and follow you each and every day.

Abundant Blessings forever,
JoAnne Malbrough
Author

Bible Versions and their Abbreviations

Amplified Bible [AMP]
Amplified Bible Classic Edition [AMPC]
American Standard Bible [ASB]
Berean Study Bible [BSB]
Common English Bible [CEB]
Contemporary English Version [CEV]
Christian Standard Bible [CSB]
English Standard Version [ESV]
Free Bible Version [FBV]
Good News Bible [GNB]
Good News Translation [GNT]
God's Word Translation [GWT]
King James Version [KJV]
Message Bible [MSG]
New American Standard Bible [NASB]
New English Translation [NET]
New International Version [NIV]
New King James Version [KJKV]
New Living Translation [NLT]
The Passion Translation [TPT]

Printed in the United States
by Baker & Taylor Publisher Services